I Wonder W...

QUESTIONS & ANSWERS ABO

SCIENCE

— AND —

TECHNOLOGY

KING*f*ISHER

KINGFISHER
An imprint of Kingfisher Publications Plc
New Penderel House, 283-288 High Holborn,
London WC1V 7HZ

Material in this edition previously published by Kingfisher in the I Wonder Why
series.

This edition first published by Kingfisher 1998
10 9 8 7 6 5 4 3 2 1
This edition copyright © Kingfisher Publications Plc 1998

A CIP catalogue record for this book is available from the
British Library.

ISBN 0 7534 0277 7

I Wonder Why series:
Editor: Clare Oliver, Brigid Avison, Jackie Gaff, Clare Llewellyn
Design: David West Children's Books
Additional design: Smiljka Surla
Art Editor: Christina Fraser

Questions & Answers About Science:
Assistant Editor: Christian Lewis
Cover design: Mike Smith

Contents

Communication

39 Can clothes keep you feeling fit?

40 How can you fit 1,000 books in your pocket?

41 Which computer was as big as a bus?

41 Who was Mr Biro?

42 Can a robot play the piano?

43 Where do people mix music?

43 Can you be an entire orchestra?

44 Why do we communicate?

45 How do we communicate?

46 When did a picture first tell a story?

46 What can a window teach you?

47 Why did knights have coats of arms?

48 What is a dead language?

48 Who started talking?

49 Do languages change?

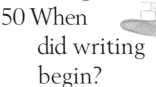

50 When did writing begin?

50 Who wrote on plants?

51 Who wrote in secret code?

51 Why did typewriters drive you crazy?

52 Why does the telephone ring?

53 How can glass link the world?

53 Are phone lines just for voices?

54 How does my stereo play a CD?

55 Who sent the first radio broadcast?

Methods of transport

Construction

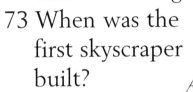

What is science about?

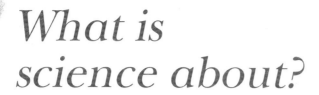

Science is all about discovering how and why things happen in the world around you. It's about everyday things like finding out where water goes when it boils, as well as more complicated things like why we need water to live.

3 Put some water in the freezer and leave it for an hour or two. What do you notice when you take it out? The water isn't liquid any more – it's a solid, and you can't pour solids.

2 Now fill a jug with water and pour it into a cup. Most liquids will pour, but some move faster than others. Try pouring some honey into a saucer – does it move as quickly as water?

1 The kitchen is a great place for scientists. Start by turning on a tap and looking at the water that flows out. Runny things like water are called liquids.

What do scientists do?

One of the first things scientists do is to ask questions. Then they try to answer the questions by looking closely at things and testing out their ideas. We call this experimenting. Scientists sometimes manage to come up with the answers – but not always!

4 All liquids can change shape, but most solids can't. Pour some water into a jelly mould and it will fill up all the nooks and crannies. What happens when you put ice cubes in?

5 Ask a grown-up to put a cup of water into a saucepan and boil it for you for 5 minutes. Lots of steam comes off, doesn't it? Let the water cool, then pour it back into the cup. There's less water now – where has the rest gone?

6 When water boils, it changes from a liquid into a gas called water vapour. We can't see this gas, so it looks as though the water has disappeared.

Why do I run out of energy?

• When you run, the stored energy in your body is changed into movement energy.

You run out of energy because you use it! Walking, running and jumping all need energy – without it you wouldn't be able to talk, write, read or even sleep! Energy is stored inside your body and comes from your food. That's why you get hungry – your body is telling you to put back some of the energy you've used.

• Lots of things give out energy, in many different forms. Here are just some of them.

Fire = heat energy

Bike = movement energy

Drum = sound energy

● Eating a small apple gives you enough energy to sleep for half an hour.

● Energy is never made or destroyed. It just changes from one form to another. Bending a bow stores energy in the bow. This changes into movement energy as the arrow flies from the bow.

What is energy?

Energy makes things happen – nothing in the universe would work without it. You can't see energy, but you can see what it does to things around you. Because of energy, cars move and planes fly, lamps give out light, drums make music, and fires give off heat.

Food = chemical energy

Train = electrical energy

Torch = light energy

Why does the spoon get hot when I stir my cocoa?

Heat energy never stays still. It is always moving. The teaspoon warms up when you stir your cocoa because heat energy is moving from the hot drink into the spoon.

● Things that allow heat to pass through them easily are called conductors. A metal spoon is a good conductor.

● Our bodies give off heat all the time. Some burglar alarms work by picking up the heat given off by a burglar's body.

Why is sunlight warm?

Sunlight is warm because the Sun gives off heat as well as light energy. The Sun's heat energy travels towards us in invisible straight lines called heat rays. You can't see them, of course, but you can feel them on your skin on hot sunny days.

● You get cold feet when you stand on a tiled floor because the tiles carry heat energy away from them. Your feet feel warmer on a carpet because it doesn't carry heat away as well as the tiles do.

How do hang-gliders hitch lifts?

When the Sun heats the land, the land then warms the air above it. Warm air is lighter than cold air, and it rises up into the sky. Hang-gliders use this rising warm air to help them to fly. The rising currents of warm air are called thermals.

Why do I feel cold after a shower?

Your body is always giving out heat. When you're wet, your body heat turns some of the water on your skin into the gas water vapour. This change from a liquid to a gas is called evaporation.

You begin to feel shivery after a shower because evaporation uses up heat.

● When you dry your hair with a hair drier, you are heating the water in your hair until it evaporates.

What makes bathroom mirrors fog up?

After a shower, the air in the bathroom is warm and steamy. When it hits a cold surface such as a mirror, the air cools down and changes back into tiny water droplets. These then fog up the mirror. The change from a gas into a liquid is called condensation.

● After a chilly night, you may see tiny drops of dew sparkling on spiders' webs or grass. Dew comes from water vapour in the air. If air cools down enough during the night, water vapour condenses to form dew.

● Condensation is a real problem for dentists. When your warm breath condenses on a hand mirror, it fogs it up and stops the dentist from seeing inside your mouth!

What can walk on water?

Tiny insects called pond-skaters are so light that they can walk across water without sinking into it! But even pond-skaters wouldn't get anywhere without a force called surface tension. This pulls on the surface of the water, making a thin stretchy 'skin' on the top.

● Raindrops aren't quite round – they're almost flat underneath.

Why are water droplets round?

Small drops of water are almost perfectly round because they are pulled into this shape by surface tension. Bigger drops spread out, though – they're too heavy for surface tension to work so well.

● The Jesus Christ lizard runs so fast that it can cross rivers and lakes without sinking – a brilliant way to escape from danger!

● Gently touch a drop of water with a soapy straw, and see how the drop gets flatter. This is because soap weakens the surface tension of water – it can no longer pull the drop into a neat round shape.

Why does soap make bubbles?

Adding soap to water weakens the pull of the surface tension, and makes the surface of the water much stretchier. It spreads out enough for you to blow air inside – it's a bit like blowing up balloons with water.

What is sound?

Sound is a type of energy. It happens when something shakes or moves back and forwards really quickly. The shaking movements are called vibrations. You hear sounds because vibrations travel through the air into your ears.

● Some singers can sing a note which is so high and so loud that it breaks a glass!

● Here's a way to see how sounds vibrate. Tie a piece of thread to some tissue paper. Now, put on some loud music and hold the thread in front of a loud-speaker. The vibrations should make the tissue paper shake. If they don't, turn up the music!

● Crashing a pair of cymbals together makes them vibrate, sending out ringing sounds.

Why do trumpeters blow raspberries?

Blowing raspberries is the only way to get sounds out of a trumpet! It makes a trumpeter's lips vibrate, and this makes the air inside the trumpet shake, too. The air comes out the other end as a musical note!

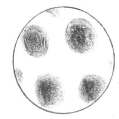

● Sound travels through air at 340 metres per second. That's nearly the length of four football pitches.

Can sound travel under water?

● Sound needs something to travel through – air, water, or some other material. There's no air in space, so astronauts have to use radios to talk to one another.

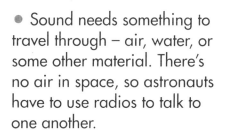

Yes, it can! Sound moves four times faster through water than through air. It can travel such long distances that whales can hear each other when they are over a hundred kilometres apart.

Why do shadows happen?

Light travels in straight lines called rays. When the rays hit something that they can't shine through, the light is blocked, and a dark shadow forms on the other side.

• There are lots of things that light can't shine through – walls, furniture, your own body, for example. We call these things opaque.

• Try to make animal shadows on a wall by wiggling your fingers in the beam of a bright torch.

• Light is another kind of energy. Plants use the energy in sunlight to make food for themselves in their leaves. Sunflowers get all the sunlight they can by turning to face the Sun as it moves across the sky.

- Did you know that you can use shadows to tell the time? Next time it's sunny, stand a pencil inside a cotton reel on a piece of paper. Every hour, draw a line along the pencil's shadow, and write down the time. Now you can use your shadow clock to tell the time on every sunny day.

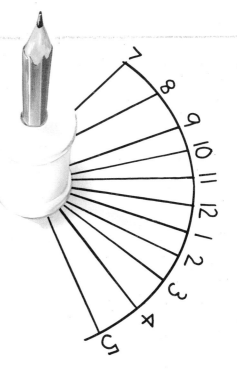

Why can I see through glass?

You can see through glass because it's transparent – that means it's clear, and it lets the light shine through. Glass is great for windows because it lets sunlight into a room, and allows you to see what's going on in the world outside!

- Bathroom windows are often made of frosted glass. This still lets some light through, but the frosting stops people from seeing straight through the glass.

Can light bounce?

When rays of light hit something that they can't shine through, they bounce off it – just like a ball bouncing off the ground. This is called reflection. We are able to see things because light is reflected off them into our eyes.

● You can see yourself when you look down into a puddle because the smooth water reflects the light straight back into your eyes.

● Up periscope! A submarine officer looks through a periscope to see what's happening above the water. Mirrors inside the periscope reflect light from things above the water straight down into the officer's eyes.

● The Moon reflects light from the Sun. It has no light of its own.

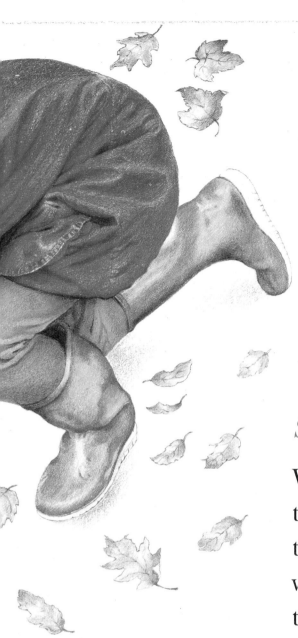

● See what happens when light passes through a single drop of water. Cut a hole in a piece of card and stick clear tape over the top. Carefully put a drop of water on the tape and look through it at something small, like a ladybird. It will make it look bigger.

Why do my legs look shorter under water?

When light enters water, its rays travel more slowly than they do through the air. This changes the way we see things. Looking down through the water in a swimming pool, your legs look very short and dumpy. Don't worry – they aren't really!

● As light passes through water, it changes the way we see things. This makes it tricky to net fish – they aren't where they appear to be. To catch one, you have to aim below the place where you actually see it.

Why do rainbows happen?

Although sunlight looks white, it's really made up of lots of different colours. During a shower of rain, the Sun sometimes shines through the tiny raindrops that fall through the air. When this happens, the water makes the light spread into all its different colours. The colours always appear in the same order, and a beautiful rainbow forms in the sky.

Card　Torch beam

Reflected light

Mirror

● Another way to see a rainbow is to hold a mirror in a shallow dish of water. Try to bounce sunlight or torchlight off the mirror on to a piece of white card. The water should make the light spread out into a rainbow.

● You don't have to wait for rain to see a rainbow. Water the garden on a sunny day, and you may see rainbow colours in the spray.

Why is grass green?

We see things when light reflects off them into our eyes. But not all of white light's colours are reflected. Some are soaked up. Grass looks green because it soaks up all the colours in white light apart from green.

● The bright colours of many animals often work as a warning. The black and yellow stripes on a wasp warn us – and other animals – to keep away from its poisonous sting.

Can cats see in colour?

● Many animals don't really need to see in colour. They rely far more on their sharp hearing and sense of smell.

Yes, they can – but they don't see all the colours that you do! Cats don't really need to see bright colours, as most of them are busiest at night, outdoors hunting for food.

What is air made of?

Air is a mixture of gases – mostly nitrogen and oxygen, with a little bit of carbon dioxide and some water vapour. It also has tiny bits of salt, dust and dirt. You can't see, smell or taste the air, but you can feel it when the wind blows.

● You're using air when you take a deep breath and blow out the candles on a cake!

● We don't notice it, but the air around us is heavy, and pushes down on us. The air in a medium-sized room weighs as much as 70 cans of baked beans!

How do bubbles get into fizzy drinks?

The bubbles in fizzy drinks are made of carbon dioxide. The gas is squashed into the bottle so hard that it disappears into the drink. When the bottle is opened, the bubbles have room to escape and start fizzing into the air.

● Make your own bubbles of carbon dioxide gas by adding a teaspoon of baking powder to a beaker of water. Stand by for the fizz!

Why do cakes rise?

When you put a cake in the oven, the mixture heats up and makes bubbles of carbon dioxide. These grow bigger in the heat, and make the cake rise.

● The air you beat into a cake mixture also helps to make the cake deliciously light.

Why do we need air?

All the animals on Earth need to breathe the oxygen in air to stay alive – and that includes you! That's because bodies use oxygen to make energy for living and growing.

● All plants need air, light and water to live and grow. So do people, and every other living thing on our planet.

● Even though they live in the sea, whales breathe oxygen from the air. Sperm whales can hold their breath for up to two hours before coming up for air.

Why do we need light?

Without the Sun's light, there would be nothing to eat! Plants are the only living things that can make their own food, and they need sunlight to do this. Everything else on Earth feeds on plants, or on plant-eating animals. If there weren't any plants, we'd all starve to death!

- If you've ever been camping, you'll know that the grass beneath a tent goes pale and begins to die. This is because it can't get the sunlight it needs to stay alive. Don't worry, it soon recovers!

Why do we need water?

It's hard to imagine, but more than two-thirds of your body is made of water. And the same is true for most other animals and plants. All of the living things on Earth need water to stay alive. Without it, they would die.

- You can survive for many weeks without food. But without water you'd last just three or four days.

Why do people invent things?

Inventors try to solve problems. They think about people's needs, and come up with an answer. When an inventor noticed how inconvenient big umbrellas were, he invented a folding one that would fit in a bag.

Gone to buy some glue!

• Post-it notes were invented by accident when someone made a glue that didn't stick properly. You could stick down a piece of paper, peel it off, and then re-stick it!

• From the moment you wake up you're surrounded by inventions. Pillows, light bulbs, and even cornflakes all help to give us an easier, comfier life.

• Some inventions are just for fun. The first Frisbees were empty pie tins belonging to a baker called Joseph Frisbie. When some of his customers tossed the tins to each other in the park, the idea for the Frisbee was born.

● Safety pins were introduced almost 200 years ago, but have a much longer history. Their inventor copied the idea from clasps worn by the Ancient Egyptians.

Inventions

● An invention is something new like a paper-clip, which never existed before someone thought of it. Things like coal and rubber weren't invented. They were already in the world. When people discovered the juice of the rubber tree they used it to make rubber. Later, rubber tyres for cars and bicycles were invented.

Where do inventors get their ideas?

Inventors get ideas for their inventions in lots of different places. Some of them study plants and animals to see how they have solved their problems. Others look at ideas from other places or from the past. Very few ideas come out of the blue.

● Burdock seeds are covered with tiny hooks that stick to things, but can be pulled off. An engineer who noticed this used his discovery to make Velcro for fastenings.

What did people use before fridges?

Electric fridges were invented around 1920. Before then, people kept their food in a wooden cupboard called an icebox. Huge blocks from the ice man kept the cupboard cold.

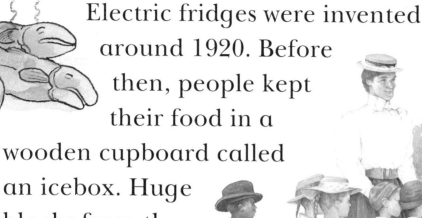

● Coca-Cola didn't start out as a fizzy drink. An American chemist called John Pemberton invented it as a sweet syrup in 1885. Soda water was added to it later.

Who ate the first cornflakes?

Two brothers, Will and John Kellogg, invented cornflakes by accident, when they were trying to make a new type of bread. One day, they overcooked a pan of wheat, rolled the mixture flat, and then watched it dry into flakes. They toasted the flakes and tasted them – delicious!

● The ice man called several times a week to deliver large blocks of ice for the icebox.

● Long ago, people made natural fridges by lining caves and holes with a thick layer of snow in winter. These ice houses kept fresh food cool right through the warm summer months.

● In 1853, a new food was invented. When a diner asked for extra-thin chips, the chef came up with the first potato crisps.

How were drinking straws invented?

One hot summer in the 1880s, a man called Marvin Stone made the first paper straw. He'd noticed that people kept drinks cooler by not touching the glass and using a hollow grass stalk to suck up the liquid.

What were the first cars like?

The first cars were steam engines on wheels – noisy, smoky machines that scared other road-users! But these steam cars soon got quicker and easier to drive. They were used for nearly 30 years, until they were replaced by faster cars with petrol engines.

● In the 1930s, planes carried 20 passengers at the most. By the 1970s, the new jumbo jets could seat up to 500! Soon, new super-jumbos will carry as many as 850 people!

How do you ride on air?

People ride on air every time they travel on a hovercraft. The hovercraft was invented by Christopher Cockerell in 1959. He discovered that trapping a cushion of air beneath a boat lifts it up above the waves, allowing it to travel much faster.

- The penny-farthing bicycle was invented in the 1860s. It had two wheels – one very large and one very small – and was named after two British coins of the time – the large penny and the tiny farthing.

- Eveyone knows about seat belts for people to wear, but did you know that cats and dogs can wear them too? So clunk-click, Rover/Felix!

- The first cars weren't allowed to go faster than 3 km/h. And someone had to walk in front with a flag to warn other road-users!

Which bikes have sails?

The fastest superbikes have solid wheels and flat frames that work in the same way as a sail. As the bike zooms along, its wheels and frame catch the wind, which helps to push the bike forward – just as it does on a boat. But most of the power still comes from turning the pedals!

Why does my watch tick?

More than 20 tiny wheels are packed neatly inside your watch. You can hear them tick and tock as the teeth of one wheel lock into the teeth of the next. The moving wheels keep time, and slowly turn the hands around the watch face.

How did people manage before clocks?

Before clocks were invented, people judged the time by looking at the Sun. They got up at sunrise, and went to bed when it was dark. They ate lunch when the Sun was up above, and ate dinner when it set in the west.

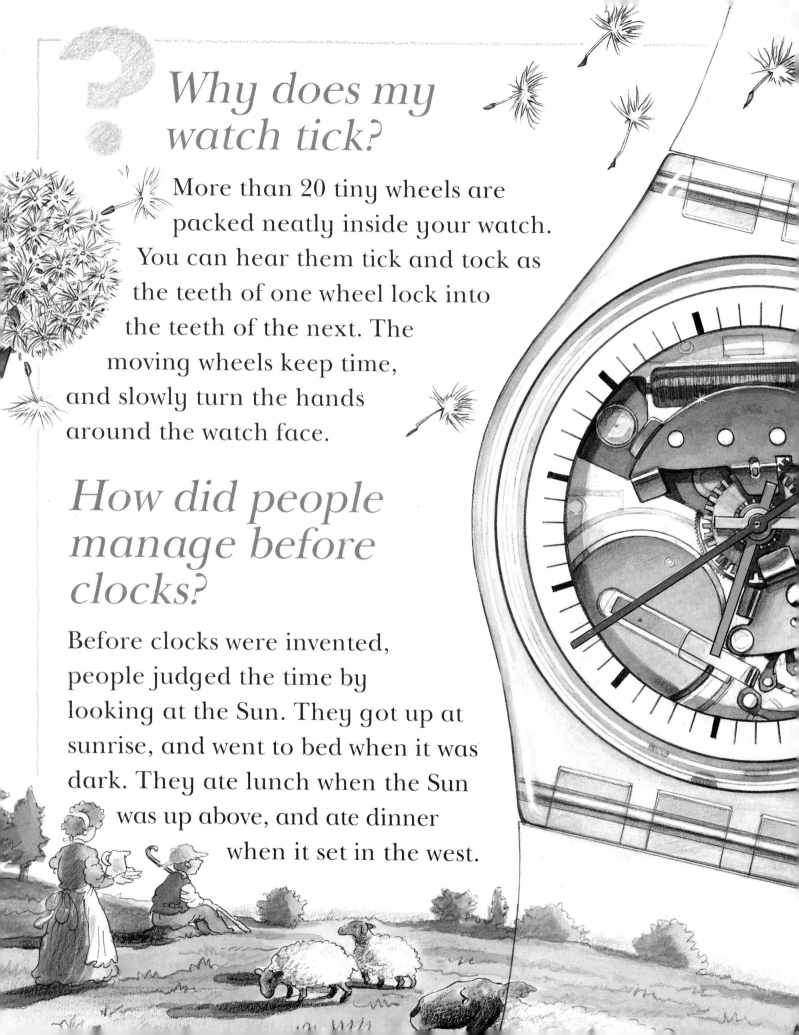

● Sailors usually work for four hours at a time. Bells ring every half an hour – one after half an hour, two after an hour and so on. When eight bells sound, the shift is over, and the sailors can take a well-earned rest.

How does a grandfather keep good time?

A tall grandfather clock has a long pendulum that swings back and forth in a steady rhythm. With every swing, wheels inside the clock slowly turn, moving the hands round the face. Winding the clock with a key stops it slowing down.

● Sundials are one of the oldest kinds of clock. Instead of a moving hand, they have a shadow, cast by the Sun. As the Earth turns during the day, the 'hand' moves around the clock.

Who took hours to take a photo?

A Frenchman called Joseph Niépce took the first-ever photograph in 1826. He had to wait eight hours before the picture was captured on a thin metal plate coated with a sort of tar. The photo was of the view from his window.

● Niépce would have found it hard to believe, but today's Polaroid cameras can produce a picture in seconds!

● In the late 1800s, it took so long to take a photo that sitters needed a back-rest to help them sit still!

When could you watch pink TV?

The first TV had an odd picture – bright pink and very fuzzy! But its inventor, John Logie Baird, had used very odd equipment to build it, including a bicycle light and a knitting needle!

The world's smallest radio is about the size of a pea!

Who invented the personal stereo?

A Walkman is a personal cassette player with headphones, which is light enough to carry around. It was invented in 1979 by a Japanese electrical company called Sony.

● The first telephone service started in 1878, in a small town in the USA. Only 20 people had phones, so they could only ring up each other!

Who invented raincoats?

The first waterproof raincoats were made in 1823 by Charles Macintosh – which is why they are often called macs. He made the cloth waterproof by sandwiching a layer of rubber between two lengths of cotton. The coats kept people dry all right, but they weighed a ton and smelt awful when they got wet!

● A lot of today's rainwear is made of PVC. It's a plastic-backed material which comes in lots of bright colours.

● It rains so much in Scotland that hill farmers buy raincoats for their sheep!

Why do zips have teeth?

Without their teeth, zips couldn't open or close. The two rows of teeth are joined by a slider, which locks them together or pulls them apart. Zips were invented in the 1890s, and were a great improvement on fiddly buttons and hooks and eyes.

• The first jeans were made by Levi Strauss for gold miners in the USA. He made them in a hard-wearing blue cloth that was used to make tents. These days it's better known as denim.

Can clothes keep you feeling fit?

Some clothes can do amazing things. You can even buy tights full of health-giving vitamins, which are usually only found in fresh fruit and veg!

• When Thomas Hancock invented elastic in 1820, he thought it would be useful along the top of pockets to stop thieves. It was someone else who realized it would be just right for holding up people's underwear!

How can you fit 1,000 books in your pocket?

There's room for about 1,000 storybooks on a CD-ROM – a small compact disc that's as thin as your fingernail and can fit in a pocket. Words, pictures and sounds can all be stored on CD-ROMs, but they only work with a computer, so you can't read one on the bus – yet!

● The Egyptians were one of the first peoples to write with ink. They made it by mixing black soot with sticky tree sap.

● Just like dinosaurs, the typewriter will soon be extinct. It was a new invention in 1873, but has now been replaced by computers and word-processors.

● Felt-tip pens went on sale in Japan in 1962. Their inventor hoped that the pen's soft tip would make people's handwriting more graceful – like the brushstrokes in Japanese calligraphy.

● Today's pocket calculators can carry out calculations much quicker than you can move your fingers. They are as powerful as the huge computers of the 1960s.

Which computer was as big as a bus?

The first computer was about as long as four buses and was called Colossus. It was built in Britain and was switched on in 1943. Very few people knew about it at the time, because one of its first jobs was to crack secret codes in the war.

Who was Mr Biro?

Ladislao Biro invented the ballpoint pen in 1938. It contained a tube of long-lasting, quick-drying ink, which rolled evenly onto the paper thanks to a tiny ball at the tip. Although Biro called his pen a ballpoint, most people now call their ballpoint a biro!

Can a robot play the piano?

A clever Japanese robot called WABOT-2 can whizz its fingers over a keyboard much faster than a human can. It can either read new music, or choose a song it has played before and stored in its memory. The cleverest thing about WABOT-2 is its sensitive fingers. It can play gently or furiously.

● WABOT-2's head is like a camcorder. As the robot reads music, the camera 'films' what it sees and stores it in its memory to play again.

Where do people mix music?

In a recording studio, the voices and instruments are recorded separately. The producer mixes the parts together on a machine called a mixing desk. He or she checks the sounds are balanced and every part can be heard clearly.

● Drum machines make the sound of all sorts of drums – but they're only as big as a chocolate box. Some of them have pads to tap out your rhythm on.

● You can record any sound you like on a sampler – even a dog's bark. You put the sounds you've sampled into tunes as if they were musical notes.

Can you be an entire orchestra?

Synthesisers are machines that can make the sound of every instrument in the orchestra. One minute they sound like a flute, the next they sound like a violin. They'll even play a simple drum pattern to give your music a beat.

Why do we communicate?

Communication is all about swapping information. If we didn't share our discoveries, we would have to learn everything from scratch. We'd have no way of knowing that fire burns, for example, until we'd been hurt. And there'd be no such thing as a favourite book! Most of all, sharing our feelings with other people makes life more enjoyable because we can have friends.

● Pictures are a good way of showing information. They can be understood by people who can't read, or who come from another country and don't know the language.

● Even before we learn how to speak, we can let others know when we want something!

Communication

● Burying a time capsule is a way to communicate across the centuries. Hopefully, it will help people in the future to piece together a picture of the past. What would you bury to show what your life is like?

● To communicate, we use our voices and our body language. When someone is a long way away, they can get in touch on the telephone or send us a letter. But people we have never met communicate with us too – in the books they write, or through films and television.

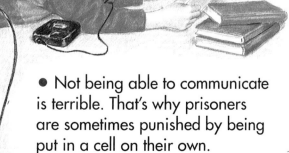

● Not being able to communicate is terrible. That's why prisoners are sometimes punished by being put in a cell on their own.

When did a picture first tell a story?

Over 20,000 years ago! Prehistoric people painted pictures on cave walls to tell stories – of a hunt, for example. And these paintings tell us a story too. They tell us that prehistoric people could make paint from earth, charcoal and plants.

What can a window teach you?

Stained-glass windows are used in churches to show scenes from the Bible. Long ago, very few people could read, but they could look at the pictures and learn a story, such as the story of Noah and the Flood.

• When artists paint portraits, they often put in clues – to tell us more about the person they are painting. Francisco Goya was a famous painter. He painted himself at work, and showed his favourite brushes and colours.

Why did knights have coats of arms?

When knights started to wear helmets, it was impossible to tell who was who, especially in the thick of battle! So every knight had a coat of arms – a design which decorated his shield, his lance and even his horse! This made sure no one on his own side would confuse him with the enemy.

• Spray-paint artists are sometimes hired to brighten up whole walls in miserable parts of a city. Not all graffiti is seen as art though! Lots of money is spent every year cleaning up unwanted graffiti.

What is a dead language?

A dead language is one that no one speaks any more. Two thousand years ago, the Romans spoke Latin to one another. Although Latin is still taught in schools, it isn't anyone's native language today, so we call it dead.

UGH UH

Who started talking?

No one knows how or when people first spoke. They might have started by copying sounds around them, such as the whistling of the wind. One of the first words probably meant 'attack'. By communicating with words, humans could help each other more easily.

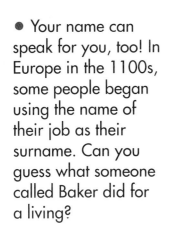

● Your name can speak for you, too! In Europe in the 1100s, some people began using the name of their job as their surname. Can you guess what someone called Baker did for a living?

● Life would be much simpler if we all spoke the same language. Hundreds of people have tried to invent one for everyone to use. Esperanto is the most popular – over 100,000 people use it!

Do languages change?

New words are being created all the time! Just think of all the new discoveries we've made during the last hundred years. Since we've been exploring space, the words spaceship, blast-off and astronaut have all been invented.

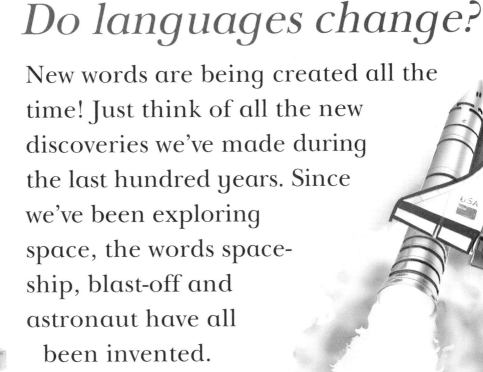

● A speech synthesiser is a special machine for people who are unable to talk. You type the words you want to say on a keyboard, and the synthesiser says them out loud for you!

When did writing begin?

The first real writing system was invented by the Sumerians over 5,000 years ago. They used small pictures called pictograms to stand for objects and ideas. Soon they invented pictograms for sounds too. Then any word that could be said could be written!

Who wrote on plants?

The Ancient Egyptians did! They used the stalks of the papyrus plant, which was found by the river Nile. They cut the stalks into thin strips, which they pressed together into sheets. Our word 'paper' comes from 'papyrus'.

• Writing probably began so that people could keep a record of money and goods.

Who wrote in secret code?

Vikings wrote using runes, which were all drawn with straight lines. The word rune means 'secret'. Very few people could read or write 1,000 years ago. Some of them even thought that anyone who could understand the runes must have magical powers!

Why did typewriters drive you crazy?

People are often scared of new inventions. When the first typewriter went on sale in 1874, some doctors said that using one could make you go mad!

• You can write on an electronic note-pad as if it were an ordinary one, but with a special pen. Some store the information exactly as you write it – others change your handwriting into neat type!

Why does the telephone ring?

The telephone rings to let you know that someone wants to speak to you! So if your friend dials your number, your phone rings out. When you answer, an electric current carries your voice along the line and your friend hears you loud and clear!

● Today, most telephone exchanges connect calls automatically with computers.

● Telephone calls used to be connected by hand. An operator asked which telephone number you wanted and plugged in the correct wire.

How can glass link the world?

Optical fibres are hair-thin strands of glass, twisted into cable. They have been laid under all the oceans and act as highways for anything from phone calls to TV programmes. Information travels along them at the speed of light.

• Telephones come in all shapes and sizes, from tiny mobiles to cartoon characters. But they all have two main parts – the transmitter you talk into and the receiver which you listen to.

Are phone lines just for voices?

Voices aren't the only things that travel along a phone line. With a videophone, you can see a picture of who's telephoning as well. With a fax, you can send letters, photos and drawings. And computers use phone lines to communicate with one another too!

• There are over 100 million telephones in the United States. In Washington DC, there are more phones than people!

How does my stereo play a CD?

The bottom of a CD may look shiny, but it is covered with billions of tiny bumps. As the CD whizzes round inside your stereo, a laser beam shines on the bumps. The beam 'reads' their pattern like a code, and then sends a message to the speakers to tell them exactly what sounds to make.

- *The Titanic* made its first and only voyage in 1912. As it sailed across the Atlantic, several other ships sent radio messages warning of icebergs ahead. The captain ignored them and the ship hit an iceberg and sank.

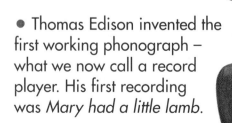

- Thomas Edison invented the first working phonograph – what we now call a record player. His first recording was *Mary had a little lamb*.

54

Who sent the first radio broadcast?

The first proper radio set that sent messages using radio waves was built by Guglielmo Marconi. But he wasn't the person who proved the waves exist – that was the scientist, Heinrich Hertz.

● Guglielmo Marconi built a machine that could produce radio waves by making a powerful electric spark.

● When a band play in a studio, the engineer records the different instruments separately. The producer mixes them together to make the song.

Which is the fastest car?

A British car called *Thrust 2* set the world land speed record in 1983. Using an aircraft jet engine in place of a normal car engine, it reached nearly 1020 kilometres an hour.

● The first car to go faster than 100 kilometres an hour was battery-powered. It was called *La Jamais Contente*, and it did this nearly 100 years ago, in 1899.

● The world's fastest sailing craft are sailboards. In good winds, they can zip across the water at more than 80 kilometres an hour.

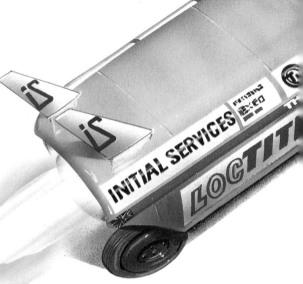

Spirit of Australia

Which is the fastest boat?

Hydroplanes skim over the water almost as if flying. In 1977, Ken Warby roared to 556 kilometres an hour in his jet-powered *Spirit of Australia*.

Methods of transport

Thrust 2

SR-71A *Blackbird*

- One of the quickest ways to travel without an engine is on skis.

Which is the fastest plane?

The fastest aircraft are planes with jet engines. The world record was set back in 1976, when the USA's SR-71A reached an amazing 3530 kilometres an hour! It was nicknamed *Blackbird*.

How far can I go in an hour?

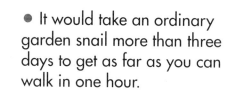

If you keep walking for an hour, and don't stop to take any rests, your own two legs will carry you about 4 kilometres. You'll be able to go farther if you run, but you'll probably have to keep stopping to get your breath back. The easiest way to travel more than a few kilometres in an hour is to get something to carry you!

● It would take an ordinary garden snail more than three days to get as far as you can walk in one hour.

● Trotting on a pony for an hour, you'd be able to travel three times as far as you would on foot.

● To walk as far as a jumbo jet can carry you in an hour, you'd have to keep going for more than ten whole days and nights!

● Racing cyclists can pedal at least ten times as fast as you can walk. They can cover as much as 40 kilometres in an hour.

● Aircraft are the fastest way to travel. Flying high above the clouds in a jumbo jet, you'd be able to get from Paris to London in less than an hour.

● Riding in a high-speed train like the Japanese Bullet train or the French TGV, you can travel at least twice as fast as you could in a car.

● Engines are more powerful than muscles, so machines can carry you much faster than legs. Riding in a car on a motorway, you can travel at more than 100 kilometres an hour!

● Even if you stay in bed all day, you will travel about 2.5 million kilometres! That's how far the Earth moves through space in 24 hours, as it goes around the Sun.

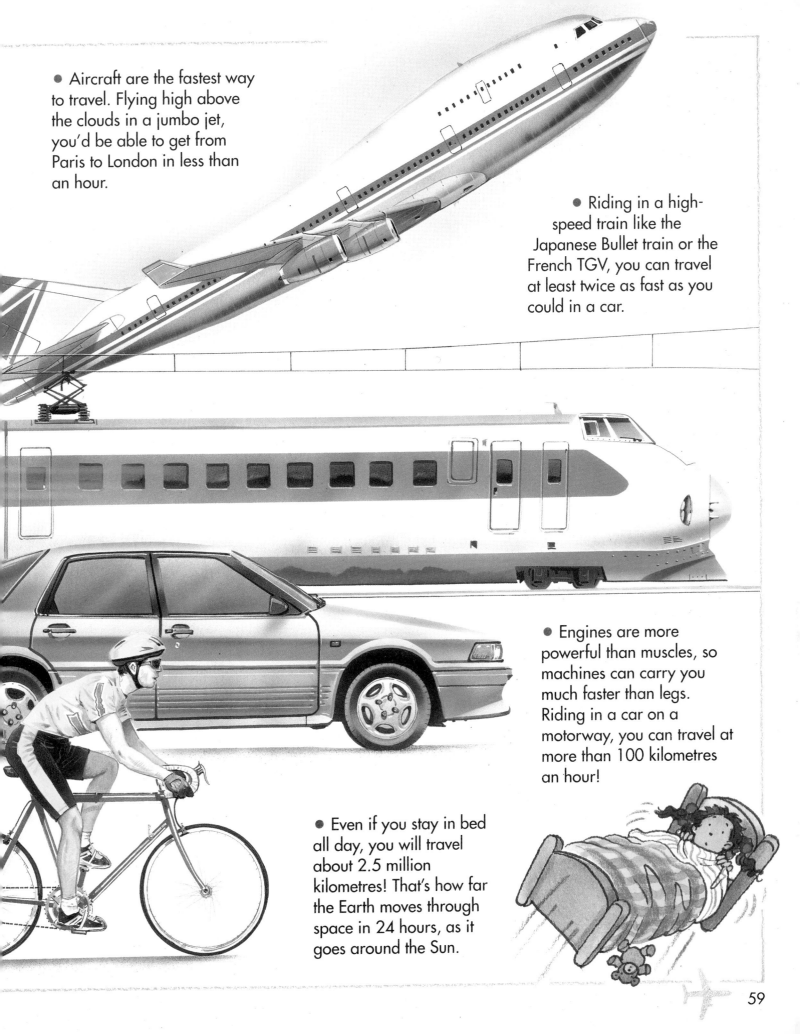

59

Which plane can waggle its nose?

The superfast passenger jet Concorde can move its nose. With its long slim nose sticking straight out, Concorde can slip through the air at well over double the speed of a jumbo jet. However, when Concorde lands, its nose has to be lowered out of the way. If this isn't done, the pilot can't see the runway!

● Concorde heats up so much in flight that its body stretches – it can get as much as 28 centimetres longer.

● The world's largest passenger planes, the Boeing 747s, are nicknamed jumbo jets after an elephant. Jumbo was a star attraction at London Zoo in the 1800s.

Can planes move their wings?

Yes, some fighter planes have wings that can be moved in and out. This is because wings that stick straight out are the best shape for taking off and landing, and for flying slowly. When wings swing back, they give the plane a smoother shape, which helps it to cut through the air at top speed.

● Birds have the best swing wings of all. A peregrine falcon holds its wings out to hover over its prey, then tucks them back to dive down for the kill. It can reach 300 kilometres an hour in its dive.

● Harrier fighter planes have been nicknamed jump jets because they can take off straight up into the air.

Why do cars need petrol?

A car needs petrol for the same reason that you need food – to give it energy to move. It's hard to tell by looking at it, but petrol has lots of energy locked up inside it. This energy is set free inside a car engine, so it can be used to turn road wheels.

- Many toy cars use electrical energy, stored in batteries. There are a few ordinary cars that run on batteries, too.

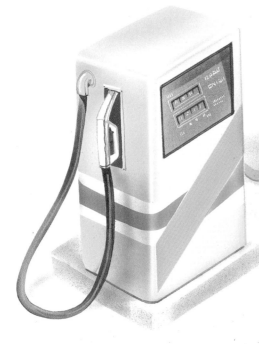

- Petrol is made from oil, and it has energy because it comes from things that were once living! Oil formed millions of years ago, from the bodies of tiny plants and animals.

Exhaust pipe

Petrol tank

- Petrol is kept in a tank. It is pumped along a pipe to the engine.

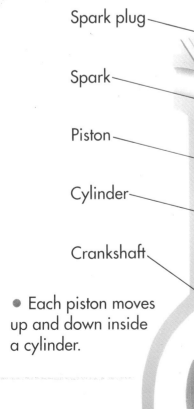

Pistons

● The world's biggest petrol station is in Jeddah, Saudi Arabia. It has over 200 pumps!

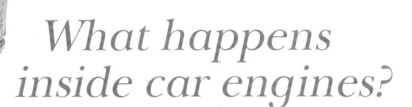

What happens inside car engines?

Petrol is mixed with air inside a car engine and then set on fire by an electric spark. This makes the air and petrol explode with a bang.

This explosion pushes engine parts called pistons up and down very quickly. The pistons make a rod called the crankshaft spin round. The crankshaft makes other rods spin, and they turn the road wheels.

Spark plug

Spark

Piston

Cylinder

Crankshaft

● Each piston moves up and down inside a cylinder.

Which are the biggest ships?

The biggest ships in the world are oil supertankers. They can be over half a kilometre long and weigh more than 1000 jumbo jets. Giant tankers can take 20 minutes to stop!

- Life jackets are only 200 years old. A French priest invented them when he lined a waistcoat with a floaty material called cork.

- Some tankers are so long that crews cycle about them!

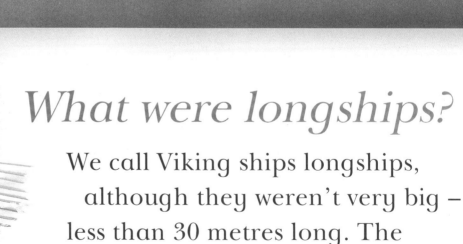

What were longships?

We call Viking ships longships, although they weren't very big – less than 30 metres long. The Vikings lived in Scandinavia about 1000 years ago. They built sturdy wooden ships and were skilful sailors.

- Viking ships could be rowed or sailed. They had a single square sail.

Which are the world's smallest boats?

Coracles are just about the world's smallest boats – they usually only have room for one person!

● Warships once had small castles front and back.

Forecastle

Sterncastle

● Ships' hammocks were first used 500 years ago. European sailors copied them from hanging beds they saw in the West Indies.

Why don't trains fall off the rails?

Trains have metal wheels and run on narrow metal rails. Metal can be very slippery, so train wheels are specially shaped to stop them falling off. The inside of each wheel has a lip called a flange, which holds it on the rail.

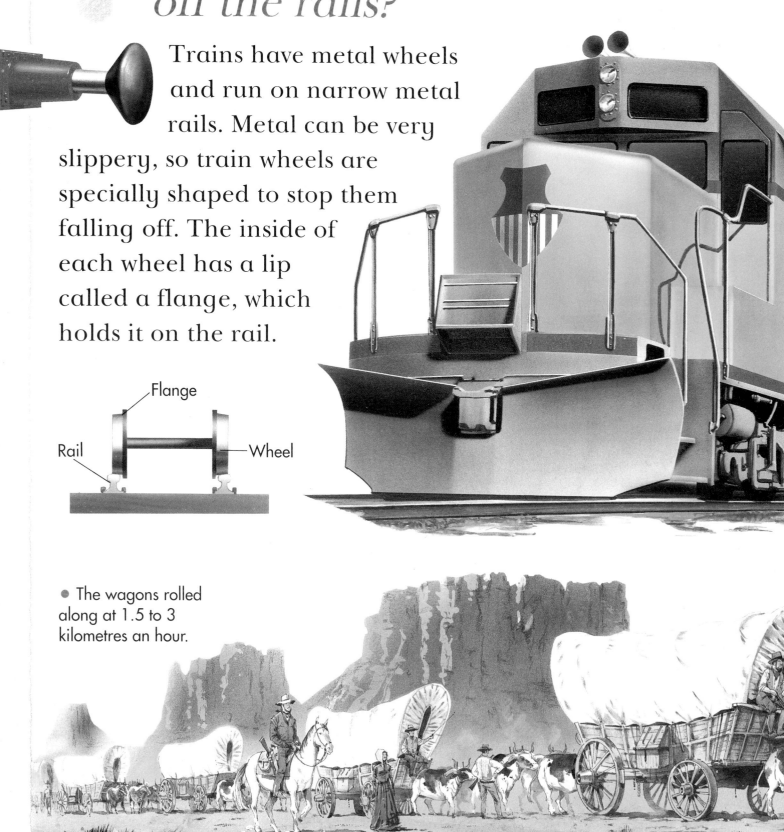

Flange

Rail

Wheel

● The wagons rolled along at 1.5 to 3 kilometres an hour.

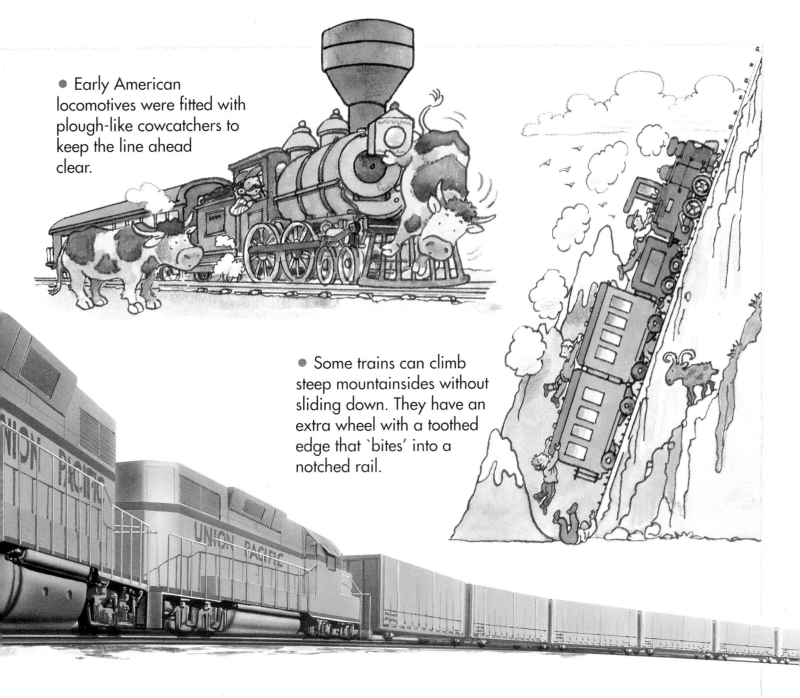

● Early American locomotives were fitted with plough-like cowcatchers to keep the line ahead clear.

● Some trains can climb steep mountainsides without sliding down. They have an extra wheel with a toothed edge that `bites' into a notched rail.

What were wagon trains?

In the 1800s, when settlers spread westward across North America, they took all their belongings with them in huge wagons drawn by oxen or mules. Families travelled in groups, their wagons following each other in a long line called a wagon train.

What are houses made from?

Most houses are made from bricks, but they can be built out of almost anything – as long as it's strong and it keeps out the weather. Builders like to use materials they can get hold of easily – bricks or stone, wood, reeds, or mud.

● Bricklayers put mortar between the bricks. Mortar is a mixture of water, sand and cement, and it glues the bricks together.

● Houses protect us from the heat in summer, and the cold and rain in winter.

● There are about 12,000 bricks in the outside walls of a two-storey house.

Construction

- There is plenty of wood in the middle of a forest for building cabins.

- In the marshes of southern Iraq, people use bundles of river reeds to build homes.

- In hot places such as Africa, people often build with mud and straw. The mixture dries hard in the sunshine.

What holds up the ceiling?

The weight of ceilings and floors is carried by strong wooden beams called joists. There are joists hidden away under the floorboards and above the ceiling of every room.

- The roof is held up by thick wooden rafters. Tiles keep out the rain.

Rafter

Joist

- Sometimes uninvited visitors live under the floor, such as the wood-eating grubs of the woodworm beetle.

What's behind the walls?

Among other things, there's usually a lot of air! That's because most brick houses have double outer walls, with a gap between the walls. Pipes and electrical wiring are tucked away in this gap.

● Building a house is teamwork. A plumber lays all the pipes, an electrician does the wiring, and a carpenter puts in the windows, doors and cupboards.

What's under the floor?

There are pipes under the floor. Some carry clean water around the house. Others take dirty water away. Some aren't for water at all – they carry gas, which is burned to heat ovens for cooking and water for washing.

Which are the world's tallest buildings?

Skyscrapers are the world's tallest buildings – but they've only held the record for 100 years or so. Before then, the world's tallest buildings were the great cathedrals of Europe.

3 The Eiffel Tower, Paris, France, 300 m high, built in 1887-89.

● In some skyscrapers, people live high above the clouds. They have to phone down to find out if it's raining at street level!

1 The Great Pyramid was built 4,500 years ago at Giza, in Egypt. It's 146 m high.

2 Before its spire fell down in 1548, England's Lincoln Cathedral topped 160 m.

● The world's tallest house of cards was well over 4 metres high – that's nearly twice as high as your bedroom ceiling.

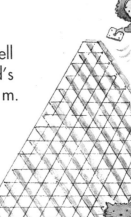

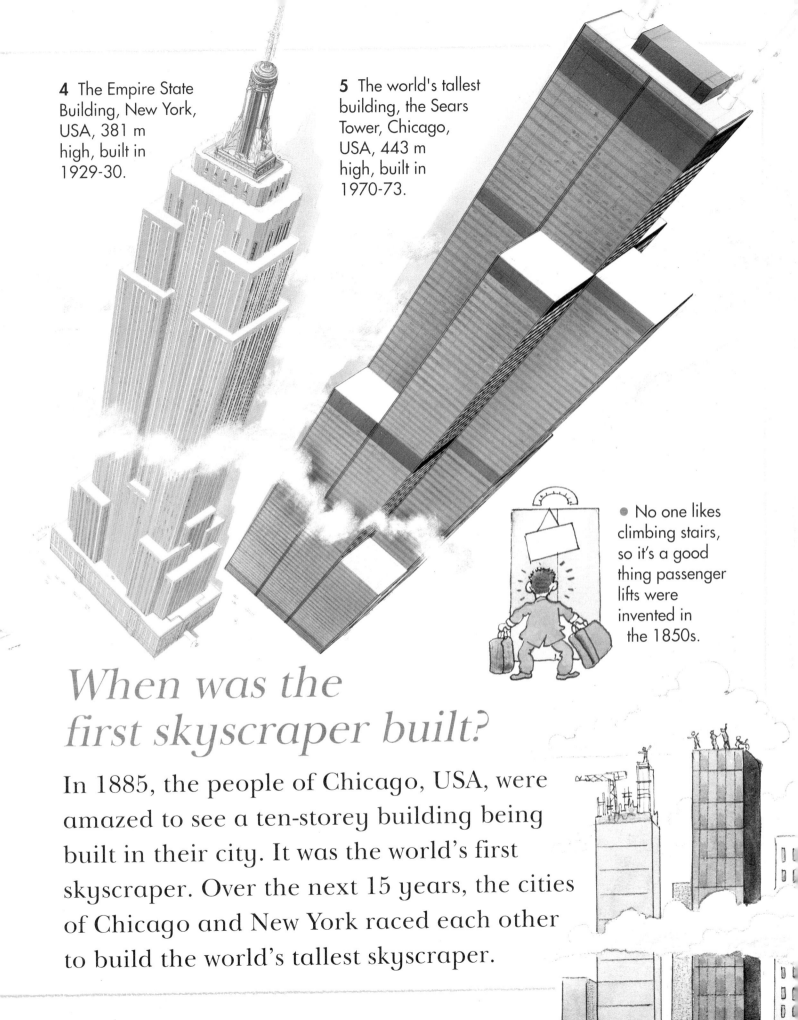

4 The Empire State Building, New York, USA, 381 m high, built in 1929-30.

5 The world's tallest building, the Sears Tower, Chicago, USA, 443 m high, built in 1970-73.

● No one likes climbing stairs, so it's a good thing passenger lifts were invented in the 1850s.

When was the first skyscraper built?

In 1885, the people of Chicago, USA, were amazed to see a ten-storey building being built in their city. It was the world's first skyscraper. Over the next 15 years, the cities of Chicago and New York raced each other to build the world's tallest skyscraper.

Which bridge can break in two?

London's Tower Bridge carries traffic over the river Thames. The roadway is built in two halves, which can be raised or lowered like drawbridges. When a tall ship sails up the river, each half of the bridge lifts up so that the ship can pass through.

● Bungee-jumpers love the Royal Gorge Bridge in Colorado, USA. At 321 metres above the surface of the river, it's the highest bridge in the world.

● Tower Bridge isn't named for its tall towers, but after its neighbour, the Tower of London.

● The Sydney Harbour Bridge is sometimes nicknamed the coathanger – you can probably see why!

● On some bridges, the whole deck lifts straight up to allow tall ships to sail beneath.

Which is the widest bridge in the world?

At 49 metres, the world's widest bridge is the Sydney Harbour Bridge, in Australia. Two trains, eight cars, a cyclist, and a person walking a dog can all travel side by side across it!

Which bridge can you shop on?

The Ponte Vecchio is lined with shops full of glittering jewellery. The bridge was built over 600 years ago, across the river Arno, in the Italian city of Florence.

Why are tunnels round?

Tunnels are round because drills make round holes! Even tunnels dug with spades have arched roofs. That's because an arch is a much stronger shape than a square. Big tunnels are carved out by tunnel-boring machines (TBMs, for short). These are like gigantic drills, twisting and grinding their way through the ground.

● The Eurotunnel TBM's cutting head has over 100 cutting rollers and 200 sharp gnashing teeth.

● The Eurotunnel between Britain and France is 50 kilometres long. If all the earth and rock from the tunnel were piled up, it would be as tall as the Eiffel Tower.

How do you tunnel through hard rock?

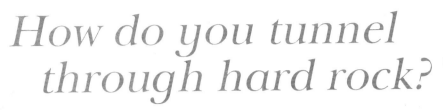

Even the most powerful TBM can't cope with really hard rock. Tunnel-builders have to use explosives to blast their way, a little bit at a time.

● Tunnels aren't just for big things like cars and trains. Smaller tunnels carry electricity cables, as well as gas, water and sewage pipes.

Can a mole dig as fast as a TBM?

A mole can dig five times faster than a TBM, using nothing but its two front paws. It's a lot smaller, though, and so are its tunnels!
You can probably guess what the TBM's nickname is – the mole, of course!

Index

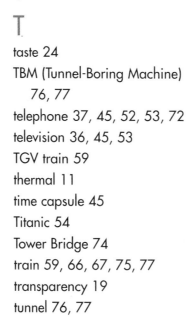

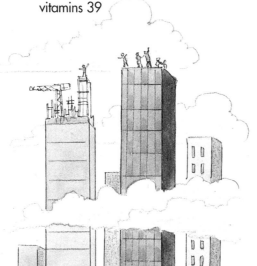